Bigger Than? Sr

Written by Margie Burton, Cathy French, and

The bee is smaller than the flower.

The dog is bigger than the kitten.

I am smaller than the tree.

We are smaller than the ball.
The ball is smaller than the tent.

The rock is bigger than I am.

The cat is bigger than the bowl.
The bowl is bigger than the fish.

We are smaller than this pool.

My head is smaller than this hat.
My hat is smaller than the umbrella.

The wall is bigger than I am.

The house is bigger than the snowman.

The baby frog is smaller than the mother frog.

The mother elephant is bigger than the baby elephant.

I am smaller than my brother.

I am bigger than my sister.

Are you big or small?